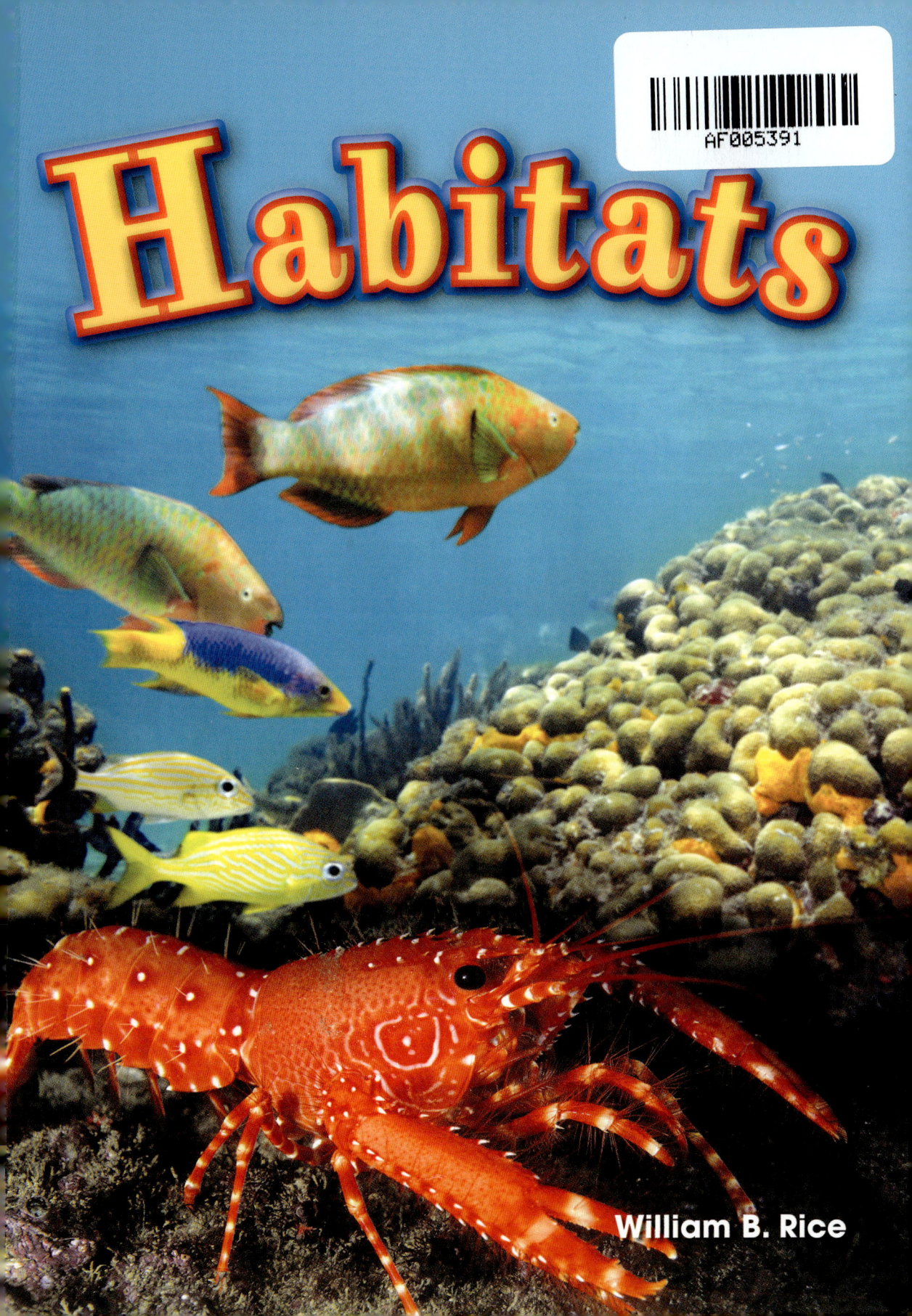
Habitats

William B. Rice

Published by Pearson Education Limited, 80 Strand, London, WC2R 0RL.

www.pearsonschools.co.uk

This edition is published by arrangement with Teacher Created Materials, Inc. for sale solely in the UK, Australia and New Zealand.

© 2015 Teacher Created Materials, Inc.

Text by William B. Rice

22 21 20 19 18
10 9 8 7 6 5 4 3 2 1

British Library Cataloguing in Publication Data
A catalogue record for this book is available from the British Library

ISBN 978 0 435 19478 9

Copyright notice
All rights reserved. No part of this publication may be reproduced in any form or by any means (including photocopying or storing it in any medium by electronic means and whether or not transiently or incidentally to some other use of this publication) without the written permission of the copyright owner, except in accordance with the provisions of the Copyright, Designs and Patents Act 1988 or under the terms of a licence issued by the Copyright Licensing Agency, Barnards Inn, 86 Fetter Lane, London EC4A 1EN (www.cla.co.uk). Applications for the copyright owner's written permission should be addressed to the publisher.

Printed in China by Golden Cup

Acknowledgements
We would like to thank the following schools for their invaluable help in the development and trialling of the Bug Club resources: Bishop Road Primary School, Bristol; Blackhorse Primary School, Bristol; Hollingwood Primary School, West Yorkshire; Kingswood Parks Primary, Hull; Langdale CE Primary School, Ambleside; Pickering Infant School, Pickering; The Royal School, Wolverhampton; St Thomas More's Catholic Primary School, Hampshire; West Park Primary School, Wolverhampton.

The author and publisher would like to thank the following individuals and organisations for permission to reproduce photographs and illustrations:
Photographs
(Key: b-bottom; c-centre; l-left; r-right; t-top; bck-background)
Cover Front: **Shutterstock**: Damsea, Back : **Shutterstock**: Amy Nichole Harris
Age Foto Stock: Spirit/Mauritius images 4b, 24-25bck, F. Hecker/ Blickwinkel 25t.
Alamy Stock Photo: Joseph Clemson 4-5bck, **Getty Images**: Pastorscott/Vetta 9t, Ifish/iStock / Getty Images Plus 19b, Sierrarat/ iStock / Getty Images Plus 20-21bck, Buccianti/ iStock / Getty Images Plus**Sciencsource**: Fletcher & Baylis 15t, NHPA 17t, Dan Suzio 22-23bck, Scott Camazine 23, Steve & Dave Maslowski 24b, **Shutterstock**: Damsea 1, Aleksey Stemmer 3br, Anton_Ivanov 5t, Pakhnyushchy 6-7bck, 6, Outdoorsman 8b, Videowokart 8-9bck, Fremme 9b,StockPhotoAstur 10-11bck, Coatesy 11t, Cbenjasuwan 11b, Filip Fuxa 12-13bck, Tolmachevr 12, Camilo Torres 13b, Skynetphoto 14b, Dmitry Pichugin 14-15bck, AustralianCamera 15b, Ethan Daniels 16b, Andrey_Kuzmin 16-17bck, Irena Kofman 18-19bck, Erik Harrison 20, Yuliya Ozeran 26-27bck, Shchipkova Elena 26b, Nickolay Vinokurov 27t, Aaltair 30, Jitchanamont 32, Baldyrgan 16c.
All illustrations: Teacher Created Materials(TCM).

Note from the publisher
Pearson has robust editorial processes, including answer and fact checks, to ensure the accuracy of the content in this publication, and every effort is made to ensure this publication is free of errors. We are, however, only human, and occasionally errors do occur. Pearson is not liable for any misunderstandings that arise as a result of errors in this publication, but it is our priority to ensure that the content is accurate. If you spot an error, please do contact us at resourcescorrections@pearson.com so we can make sure it is corrected.

Contents

What Is a Habitat?................. 4

What Makes a Habitat?.............. 8

Where Do Living Things Live?........ 16

At Home......................... 26

Let's Try It!..................... 28

Glossary........................ 30

Index........................... 31

Your Turn!...................... 32

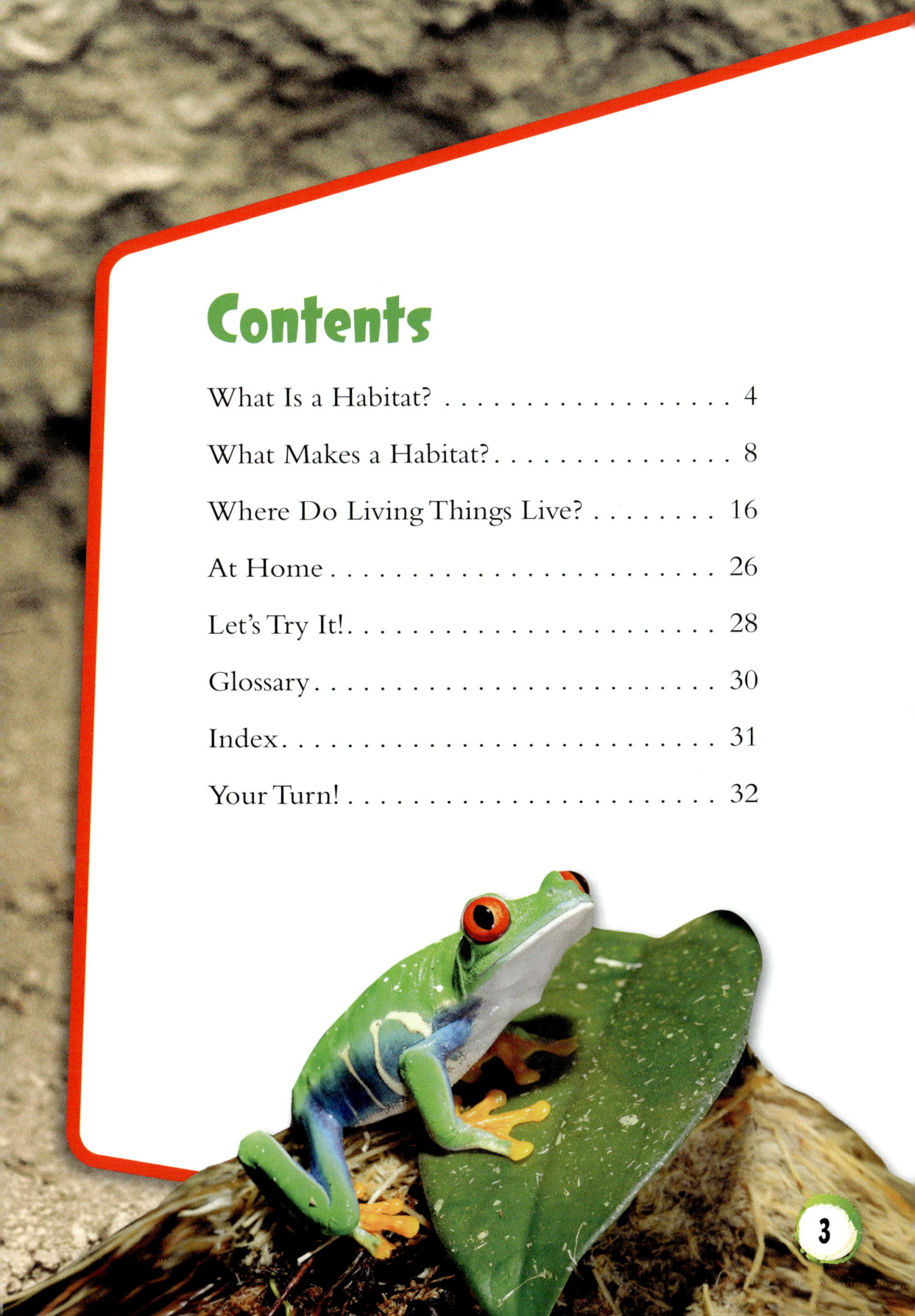

What Is a Habitat?

Imagine you're waiting at the bus stop, and see a hippo walking down the street. You'd probably be surprised. The hippo just doesn't belong on your street! Your street is not the hippo's **habitat**.

Where does a hippo belong?

The hippo's real habitat is a grassland with calm water.

A hippo's skin is red. It acts as a sunscreen to protect the hippo in its habitat.

What is a habitat? It is a home for a living thing. Every living thing has a place that is best for it. That place has what the living thing needs. It can live well there.

Starfish have many habitats. They often live on sandy shores.

What Makes a Habitat?

The right habitat for a living thing contains all that it needs to live well. This means the right soil, water, food and light. It means the right **climate** too. It also means the right predators!

Predators

Predators are animals that live by killing and eating other animals (their **prey**).

a coyote with its prey

A tree frog lives in a rainforest habitat.

Some lizards live in the desert, where they enjoy the sun's heat.

When there is the right kind of soil, plants can grow properly. Then animals can eat the plants, and other animals can eat the plant-eating animals.

Animals also need to find or make shelters. They can do this easily when they are living in the right habitat.

Plants and animals need water too. Some need fresh water, and some need salt water. All plants and animals need to live in habitats with the right kind of water for them.

This bird drinks fresh water from a river.

Badgers dig burrows in the land.

A barrel cactus grows best in sandy soil.

In autumn, chipmunks store food in their burrows to eat through the winter. This chipmunk has stored sunflower seeds in its cheeks.

Living things also need the right kind of food. Plants need **nutrients** from the soil. Plants also need **energy** from the sun. Sunlight helps them to grow.

Some animals eat plants. Other animals eat meat — and some animals eat both plants and meat. Whatever their food is, all plants and animals need plenty of the right type to live well.

This bearded dragon is about to catch a grasshopper.

The right predators?

If there are too many of one kind of animal in a habitat, there will not be enough food to go around. By eating some of the animals, predators keep animal groups from growing too large.

Over a long time, living things change to help them **survive**. Some do well in warm and dry climates. Some like to live in warm and wet climates. Some do best in cold climates.

Scorpions live in a dry desert climate.

Living things **evolve** to live in certain climates. Over a long time, their bodies change to help them survive. Some animals grow thick fur for the cold. Some plants grow deep roots to reach water. Living things have many amazing ways to survive!

Plants on the floor of the rainforest often have large leaves to absorb as much sunlight as possible.

Where Do Living Things Live?

Each living thing has a habitat that is just right for it. Here are some examples.

Lobsters

Lobsters are found in all oceans. They live on the ocean floor, mostly near the shore. They live in cracks and burrows in rocky, sandy or muddy areas. They eat sea plants and animals.

> Lobsters have hard shells to protect them. As they grow, they shed their shells and grow new ones.

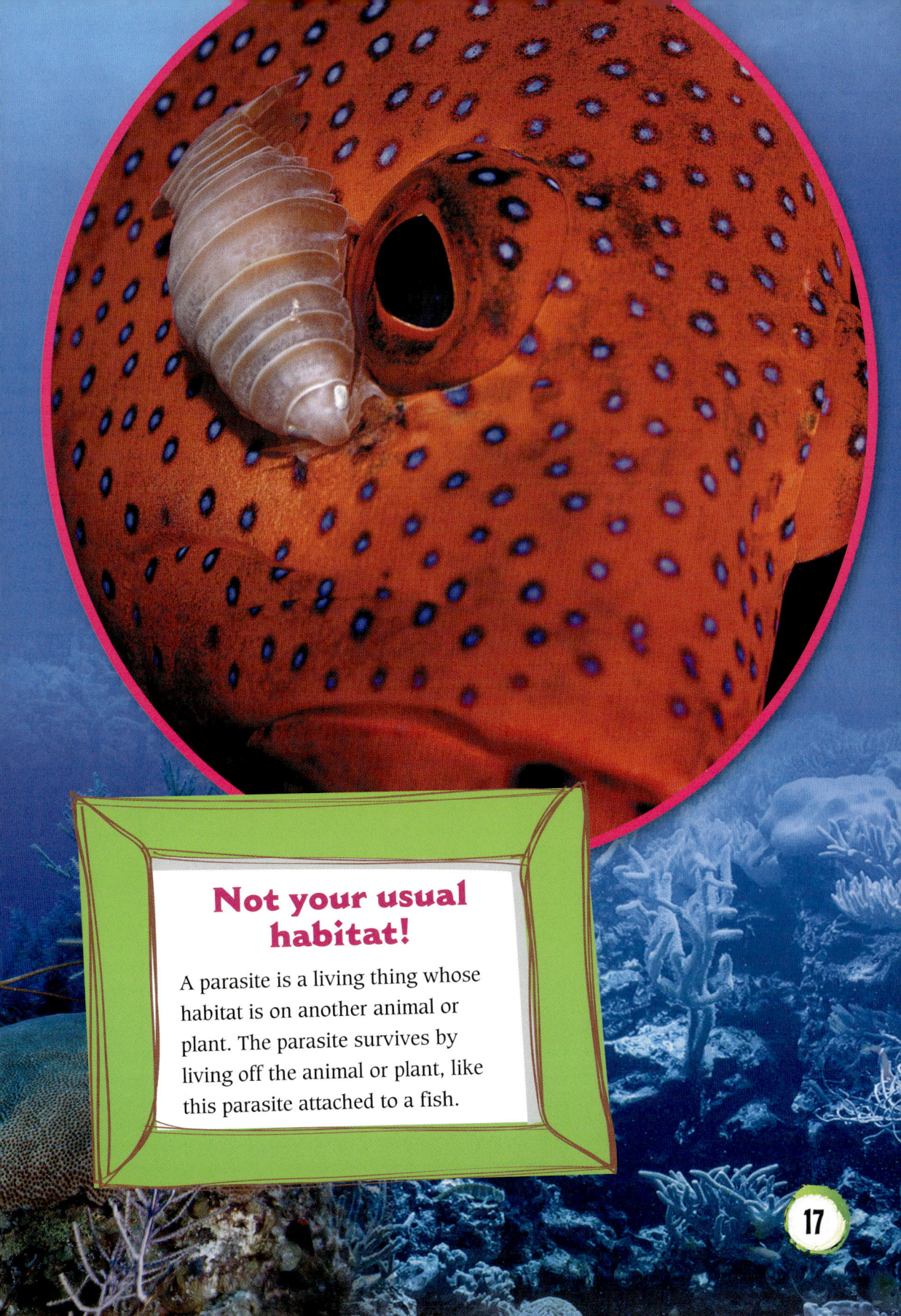

Not your usual habitat!

A parasite is a living thing whose habitat is on another animal or plant. The parasite survives by living off the animal or plant, like this parasite attached to a fish.

Brain corals are found in most of the world's oceans.

Brain corals

Brain corals are small ocean animals. They live in coral groups on the ocean floor. They like warm, shallow water. They don't move, but their food floats to them when other animals swim past and stir up the water.

Tentacles

During the day, brain corals wrap themselves in their tentacles to stay safe. At night, they reach out their tentacles to catch food.

Bristlecone pines

Bristlecone pines are tough trees. They grow high in the mountains in the dry areas of western USA. They grow slowly because it is cold and windy there. Their thick, strong wood helps to keep the trees safe from pests and diseases. They are good at getting the nutrients they need from the soil.

Bristlecone pines can live more than 5,000 years.

As old as can be

The Great Basin Bristlecone Pine is one of the oldest living organisms found anywhere on Earth.

Black widow spiders

Black widow spiders live in many places, including Australia, southern Europe and the USA. They live under and behind large objects. They like places that are dark, cool and moist. They weave webs with their sticky silk, and eat insects that get trapped in the webs.

Black widow spiders are mainly dark brown or black, with a red hourglass spot on their bellies.

This black widow spider has caught prey in its web.

Raccoons

Raccoons mainly live in forests in North America. However, they are clever animals, and they have learned to live in lots of other places too — even cities. They live in small family groups, and they eat plants and animals. They use their front paws almost like people use their hands.

Raccoons are good at finding food anywhere. They are not picky eaters.

A raccoon's paws can do many things.

At Home

Every living thing has a home, or habitat, that is right for it. Its habitat has what the plants and animals need to be healthy.

We each belong in our own habitat.

Polar bears have thick fur, which is perfect for a cold, icy habitat.

This mongoose lives where it can eat small snakes and birds.

Some elephants live in rainforests.

Let's Try It!

Can you create a habitat? Try it for yourself!

What you need

- activated charcoal
- ferns
- gravel
- large glass jar with lid
- moss
- potting soil
- water

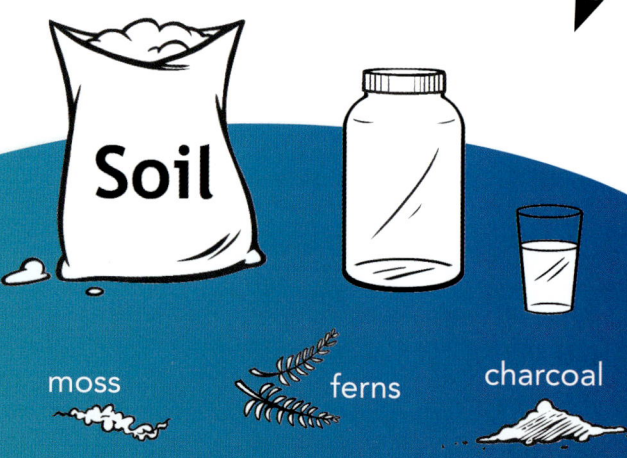

What to do

1 Cover the bottom of the jar with about two centimetres of gravel. Add a thin layer of charcoal. Add a layer of soil about five or six centimetres deep.

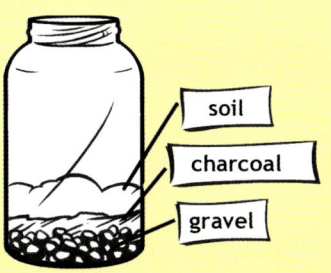

2 Plant small ferns and moss in the jar. Plant the largest plants first.

3 Water the plants just a little. Put on the lid to keep the water in. (You will need to add only a few drops of water every few months.)

4 Place the jar in natural light, but not bright sunlight. Observe your habitat. What happens to the plants?

Glossary

climate – usual type of weather a place gets

energy – power that can be used to do something

evolve – to change slowly over time to become stronger and better suited to certain conditions

habitat – place where something lives

nutrients – substances that plants, animals and people need to live and grow

prey – living things that are hunted by other living things for food

survive – continue to live

Index

climate, 8, 14–15

energy, 13

food, 8, 10, 12, 13, 18, 19, 24

nutrients, 13, 20

oceans, 16, 18

plants, 10, 13, 15–16, 24, 26, 29

predators, 8, 13

prey, 8, 13

shelter, 10

soil, 8, 10, 11, 13, 20, 28–29

sunlight, 13, 15, 29

water, 5, 8, 10, 15, 18, 29

Your Turn!

Different habitats

There are many different habitats near where you live. Look for two different habitats. How are they alike? How are they different? Draw a picture of each habitat.